THIS BOOK BELONGS TO:

....

(the 'Superstar Dog')

AND ....

....

(the 'Facilitating Human')

THE LITTLE BOOK OF
DOG TRICKS

**Easy tricks that will give your pet
the spotlight they deserve**

Julie Tottman

SEVEN DIALS

Originally published in Great Britain in 2017 by Seven Dials as *Superstar Dogs*
This edition published in Great Britain in 2018 by Seven Dials
An imprint of Orion Publishing Group Ltd
Carmelite House, 50 Victoria Embankment, London, EC4Y 0DZ

An Hachette UK Company

10 9 8 7 6 5 4 3 2 1

ISBN: 9781841883175

Cover photography: Shutterstock
Illustrations: Emanuel Santos

Printed and bound by CPI Group (UK) Ltd, Croydon, CR0 4YY

The Orion Publishing Group's policy is to use papers that are natural,
renewable and recyclable products and made from wood grown in
sustainable forests. The logging and manufacturing processes are expected
to conform to the environmental regulations of the country of origin.

Every effort has been made to ensure that the information in this book is
accurate. The information in this book may not be applicable or suitable
for every dog. People should check for themselves if the animal is able to
perform the tricks and also to ensure their own safety. If you are concerned
about the health of your pet or its ability to perform any of the actions in
the book, you should consult a veterinarian practitioner first. Neither the
publisher nor author accepts any responsibility for any personal injury or
other damage or loss arising from the use of the information in this book.

www.orionbooks.co.uk

CONTENTS

HELLO FELLOW DOG LOVER!

So long as you have praise, enthusiasm and rewards in abundance, it doesn't matter what type of dog you have or their personality: in my experience, all dogs love learning tricks. Not only do they find it fun, they love to please and feel very proud of themselves when they make you happy. It's also a great way to stimulate them and stop them getting bored, and it builds a wonderful relationship between the two of you.

I've filled this book with tricks I've been teaching dog 'actors' for the last two decades; some cute, some funny, but all impressive. All the tricks here can be taught by anyone, ranging from the downright easy – such as teaching your dog to spin (page 84) – to ones which require a little more patience and practice – such as the bring-in-the-newspaper trick (see 'Bring an object', page 111). All of them are worth the effort: I still get a thrill when a dog salutes for the first time, and my heart always melts when they master covering their eyes.

A question I am often asked is whether you can teach an old dog new tricks. You absolutely can! I have trained dogs from the age of 8 weeks up to the age of 10 years. So, whether you have a puppy or a veteran, I promise he or she can be rivalling the movie stars in no time.

Good luck!

A BIT ABOUT ME

I've been an animal trainer for film and television for over twenty years, something I still pinch myself about. Animals have always been my absolute passion; at 13 I started working in a poodle parlour on Saturdays and I did my apprenticeship there when I left school, becoming a doggy hairdresser soon after. It hadn't crossed my mind to look into animal training as a career until a friend's father – an art director in the film industry – told me the job existed. I couldn't believe it: getting paid to play with animals all day and go on film sets?! It was too good to be true.

I felt sure I didn't stand a chance of breaking into it, but I managed to find the names of some agencies through a friend in the industry and I eagerly contacted all of them. I did a lot of work for free before I finally landed a full-time job, and a few years later I was given an amazing opportunity when I was asked to work for an internationally acclaimed animal training company, Birds and Animals. I've now run the UK branch for 18 years.

One of the things I love about my job is how different each day is. At any one time, I might be working on anything between one and eight feature films, as well as adverts and TV shows, and over the years I've trained reindeer, monkeys, mongoose and bats, to name just a few. But dogs are by far the animal I've worked with the most. In fact, the film that particularly sticks out for me through the years involved lots of dogs: *102 Dalmatians*. I was the head puppy trainer, so essentially it was my job to play with adorable puppies all day! It was such an incredible experience.

Pretty much all dogs love to be trained, but – just like humans – not all dogs want to be actors. This means casting the right dog is very important. The first thing I look for is confidence. Film sets are often big places with lots of people, noise and lights, so a shy or nervous dog simply wouldn't enjoy it. The second thing all dog actors need to be is greedy! A greedy dog with lots of energy is perfect, because he or she will be motivated by the reward and will really enjoy learning and having lots to do and think about.

I try to rescue as many dogs as I can when it comes to casting. Once I have the description of the particular type of dog needed, I contact rescue centres to see if they have any that fit the bill and are in need of a home. One of my favourite dogs over the years was an eight-year-old Yorkshire Terrier named Pickles. She was in such horrendous shape when I went to collect her: she had been rescued from a puppy farm and was very sick. I nursed her back to health and, once she was better, I trained her for a film called *What a Girl Wants*, which starred Colin Firth and Amanda Bynes. She was always so happy and would do anything I asked her to do, and she loved all the attention she got. She stayed with me after the filming was over and lived until she was 20 years old. Rescue dogs often turn out to be the best dogs; most of them just need love and understanding and to have their energy channelled in a positive way. It is wonderful to give them a second chance.

HOW TO USE THIS BOOK

Hopefully you've bought (or been given) this book because you already have a dog; so long as you have one, the rest is very simple*!

☐ Have a read of 'Top tips for success' (page 13), which offers lots of advice on how to get started and teach tricks successfully.

☐ Start with the tricks in 'The Essentials' chapter – your dog needs to know these before you move on to any others.

☐ Before you begin each trick, take a look at the key at the top for the following information:

 what size dog the trick is suitable for. Measuring up to your dog's shoulder, small means 30 cm/12 inches or under, medium means 45 cm/18 inches or under, and a big dog is anything above that.

the average length of time it will take for your dog to be performing the trick perfectly on cue.

 what you'll need to successfully teach the trick.

 the tricks your dog needs to know already before you attempt the trick you're looking at.

Each time you finish a trick, sign the box at the bottom of the page. Then, when your dog has successfully completed all the tricks in the book, award him or her the coveted certificate at the very back and let your dog do a smug lap of honour around the park.

* If you don't have a dog then you can look into borrowing one using BorrowMyDoggy.com.

TOP TIPS FOR SUCCESS

The below FAQs provide some useful advice on how to approach trick training and give you and your dog the best chance of success. Give them a read-through before you get stuck into the tricks.

Q: WHERE IS THE BEST PLACE TO TEACH MY DOG TRICKS?

A: At home – somewhere familiar where your dog feels comfortable and won't be distracted by other dogs or fun places to explore.

Q: WHEN IS THE BEST TIME TO TEACH MY DOG A TRICK?

A: In the day when your dog isn't tired, and before feeding time. Do not give him or her a huge meal and then expect them to want a training session straight after – like us, they want to rest after a meal! Due to medical reasons to do with their tummies, it is absolutely crucial that larger breeds are not exercised after a meal; they should have a good couple of hours of rest.

Q: HOW MANY TRICKS CAN I TEACH MY DOG AT ONCE?

A: Two or three. Once your dog has these mastered perfectly, stop those tricks and pick a couple more. You don't want to overload your dog with too much information. Your dog won't forget the previous tricks he or she has learnt, but you should refresh them from time to time to keep the standard high.

Q: HOW SHOULD I PRAISE MY DOG? HOW MUCH FUSS SHOULD I MAKE?

A: By saying 'good' (or 'good boy'/'good girl') in a positive, animated way – the tone of your voice is key here. You can give them a stroke as well, although you may want to reserve this for when they've mastered the whole trick, rather than at the end of each little step. It's important to be very vocal with your praise in the early stages of training any trick, when your dog is trying to work out what you are asking, and once they understand and succeed. You can make less of a song and dance about it once they are doing it consistently, but never stop praising them altogether. Reassure your dog all the time during training. Never, ever scold your dog – trick training is all about the carrot, never the stick!

Q: WHEN I'M REWARDING MY DOG, DOES IT MATTER WHICH WAY ROUND I SAY 'GOOD' AND GIVE THE TREAT?

A: You should say 'good' first, then give your dog the reward. This reinforces the fact that your dog is getting the treat for what he has done correctly. For example, if you say sit and he sits, say 'good' the second he does it and then give him the treat. He will come to learn that when you say 'good' a treat is on its way.

Q: WHAT TREATS SHOULD I USE?

A: Whatever your dog's favourite treat is. I often use little bits of chicken or sausages. It's very important, however, to make sure your dog doesn't become overweight and have too much salt or fat in their diet. If you are doing lots of sessions, be aware of how much you are feeding throughout the day and alter their main meal accordingly.

Q: WHERE SHOULD I KEEP MY TREATS?

A: It's up to you, but I like to keep my treats in a bum bag. This makes it easy to reward your dog quickly. They also get to know the bum bag, so when you put it on they get super excited as they know you are about to begin a training session.

Q: IS THERE A TIME WHEN I CAN ASK MY DOG TO DO A TRICK WITHOUT GIVING A REWARD AT THE END OF IT?

A: You should always reward your dog, even for the simplest task. Once they have learnt several tricks you can ask for them in a row and then reward at the end. I also like to keep rewarding for the basic behaviours (such as sit and stay), as if these get weak it has a knock-on effect for other tricks.

Q: WHAT MOOD SHOULD MY DOG BE IN FOR THE BEST CHANCE OF SUCCESS?

A: Dogs love learning new things and being rewarded, so your dog's mood will probably pick up the second he realises he is about to be trained. However, there are a few things to think about. Like us, dogs tend to be lethargic if it's really hot, so if your dog is panting, then wait until he has cooled down. Also, if you've treated your dog to a lovely long walk or he is tired, then it's unfair to expect too much, as he may not have the energy to learn. Let your dog rest and start your lesson later.

Q: ARE THERE CERTAIN BREEDS OF DOG THAT ARE EASIER TO TRAIN THAN OTHERS?

A: All dogs are happy to be trained, but there are some breeds that show more enthusiasm and have higher energy levels. Working breeds (such as Collies, German Shepherds, Spaniels, Labradors, Poodles and Dobermans) are the easiest breeds to train.

Q: HOW DO I LET MY DOG KNOW THAT THE TRICK IS OVER?

A: By employing the release technique – 'OK' (see page 22).

FIVE FINAL TOP TIPS ...

1 **LITTLE AND OFTEN.** It is much better to do six short sessions a day than one long one. Your dog will become bored if you make it too long. Keep it fun.

2 **PRAISE, PRAISE, PRAISE.** Trick training is all about encouragement.

3 **NEVER GET CROSS!** Quite often if my dog isn't doing something right, it'll be because I'm doing something wrong. If your dog isn't understanding a command, re-read the instructions and start again another day. NEVER yell at or smack your dog. If he or she is having a cheeky day and misbehaving, simply stop the training session and ignore the naughty behaviour. This will really make him or her want to be a good boy or girl next time, as they will feel they've missed out on fun times!

4 BE CONSISTENT. Just like humans, dogs respond well to routines. Aim to keep where, when and how long your trick training sessions are consistent, as well as how you ask for a trick to be performed and how you praise a good performance.

5 END ON A HIGH. Where possible, finish on a good note when your dog has achieved the behaviour or is getting close.

THE ESSENTIALS

The following basic behaviours form the
basis of most other tricks you'll want to teach
your dog, so it's worth making sure your dog is
comfortable with doing all these first.
Once you're both happily doing these
then the sky's the limit!

THE RELEASE TECHNIQUE: OK

For all of the tricks in this book, get your dog used to knowing that the trick is over when you say the word '**OK**' excitably. Make sure you do it at the end of each session so they know they can stop doing the tricks and go off to relax or play.

SIT

| ALL | 1–3 DAYS | TASTY TREATS | – |

*This is the trick to begin all tricks! Once your dog has mastered this then the possibilities for the two of you are endless. Most dogs pick up **sit** quite quickly with repeat practice over a few days – I'd say try doing it four to six times a day. Little and often is the key when starting.*

HOW TO START

You can stand or kneel in front of your dog, depending on his size. If you have a large dog it is much easier to stand.

HOW TO DO

- Show your dog you have the treat. This will keep his attention on you. The idea is to have your dog follow a treat. Hold the treat just above his head and move it backwards straight over his head towards his tail. This should encourage his bottom to drop.

- As soon as his bottom touches the floor say 'good' and reward him immediately with the treat.

- Repeat and add the word **sit** as you raise the treat. Always be ready to give your dog quick praise when he performs the desired behaviour. Once your dog is doing this consistently, just use **sit** and your hand as a visual cue without the treat as a lure and reward once he has sat.

TIP

If your dog becomes confused and backs away after the treat rather than looking up, teach the trick against a wall.

I STARTED THIS TRICK ON: ....

I COMPLETED THIS TRICK BY: ....

STAY

| ALL | 1 WEEK | TASTY TREATS | SIT |

Teaching your dog to stay in one place is another basic trick that paves the way for lots of others – you're never going to get very far if your dog is running off every time you're asking her to do something! When you first teach her to stay, make sure you practise continuously over the course of a week, four to six times a day, so that she doesn't forget – and so you can slowly build up both the distance between you and the time you ask her to stay still for.

HOW TO START

This is always easier to teach from a sit, with you standing quite close to your dog with a treat in one hand.

HOW TO DO

- With your dog sitting, use the flat of your hand (the one that doesn't have the treat in) as a signal. Hold it up as a lollipop lady might to stop traffic, and say '**stay**'.

- You will need to build up distance between you and your dog slowly, as well as the time you ask her to sit there for. At first, as long as she stays for a second, reward her with the treat and tell her 'good'.

- Then start again and back a foot away, always keeping your hand flat and reinforcing the word **stay** every two to three seconds.

- You can then repeat and try backing even further away, waiting for a few seconds before you say 'good' and reward her with the treat.

- Keep doing this at the distance of 30–90cm/1–3ft until your dog will stay for at least 20 seconds. You can then try backing further away.

- Don't reward her with the treat if she runs to you before you ask her to – even if she stayed well beforehand – as you will only be rewarding the fact she ran to you rather than the fact she stayed. Simply ask her to sit again and start over.

- Aim to end up with a good two-minute sit-stay.

This will take time. It is best to start this in a quiet environment so as not to distract your dog – do not start in a park or field, as this is giving your dog an unfair chance of failure. Once you have a strong two-minute sit-stay you can add in distraction. Eventually you could build up to as long 10 minutes if you wanted – but this is a big ask!

TIP

Don't ask for too much from your dog too soon; the key here really is to build up time and distance slowly. Always reward your dog in the place and position you asked them to stay in to avoid confusion.

I STARTED THIS TRICK ON: ....

I COMPLETED THIS TRICK BY: ....

DOWN

| ALL | 1–3 DAYS | TASTY TREATS | SIT |

Getting your dog to lie down on cue is another trick that will enable you to do lots more together. If your dog has mastered sit, then he should find this one very easy to catch on to.

HOW TO START

Stand or kneel in front of your dog (depending on his size) and ask him to sit.

HOW TO DO

- Once your dog is sitting, hold a treat in front of his nose so that he can see and smell it.

- Take the treat towards the floor (but don't let go), saying '**down**' whilst you do this. Your dog will follow the treat and drop to the floor.

- As soon as he is in a lying-down position say 'good' and reward him quickly with the treat. Always reward your dog whilst he is still in the down position and not if he jumps up.

- Once he has mastered this, repeat the trick and back away a step or two. You can then reward him and tell him 'good' for staying there, so long as he is still down and has not got up to greet you. Once he is doing this consistently, you can just use your hand and **down** as the cue, rather than using the treat to lure him.

TIP

If your dog isn't following the treat naturally, hold the treat in one hand and lower it to the floor as a lure. With your other hand you can – very gently – press on his shoulders to encourage him towards the ground.

I STARTED THIS TRICK ON: ....

I COMPLETED THIS TRICK BY: ....

PAW

ALL 2–4 DAYS TASTY TREATS SIT

Getting your dog to put her paw in your hand is a nice easy trick to teach, and it leads on to other tricks such as 'wave' (see page 39) and 'touch object with paw' (see page 69).

HOW TO START

Ask your dog to sit and kneel or stand in front of her. Have a treat ready, but make sure it's in the hand you don't want to catch her paw with.

HOW TO DO

- Gently touch your dog's paw. Say the word '**paw**'. She should lift it very slightly. Give her a treat and tell her 'good'. If she doesn't lift it then you can pick her paw up to show her what you mean.

- Keep doing this until she lifts it high enough and you can catch it in your hand.

31

- Keeping her in a sit position, back away slightly and make the same hand gesture as when asking for her paw, whilst saying the cue, '**paw**'. As soon as she lifts it go straight in and catch it. Reward her immediately – don't reward her once it's back on the ground, the paw needs to be in your hand.

I STARTED THIS TRICK ON: ....

I COMPLETED THIS TRICK BY: ....

STAND

ALL

1 WEEK

TASTY TREATS

SIT

The trick here is to teach your dog to stand but not travel forward. This trick is useful for when you want to teach your dog a sequence of tricks – but I'd suggest leaving this until your dog is performing lots of tricks; do not try to include this too early on or you'll confuse your dog. Always reward your dog in the standing position if you have asked him to do this, and then release him by saying OK (see page 22), which lets your dog understand the exercise has been completed.

HOW TO START
Stand in front of your dog and ask him to sit.

HOW TO DO
- Whilst he is sitting, put a treat directly in front of his nose. As he leans forward to get the treat pull it away and down slightly towards the floor. His bottom should rise up.

- As soon as he lifts his bottom say '**stand**', reward him quickly with the treat and say 'good' – making sure to do this before he steps forward.

- To ask your dog to stand from 'down' position, follow the steps above but change the starting position to 'down'. Hold the treat in front of your dog's nose and then, as he leans forward to get it, pull the treat upwards. Reward in the same way.

TIP

Dogs sometimes get confused with 'stand' from the 'down' position if you do not hold the treat correctly and it is too low. Hold the treat at waist height. I stretch my arm out to the side as a visual cue.

If you have a small dog it is sometimes easier to teach this on a low table, so your dog can't move forward once standing. You can encourage the right movement by putting your hand under your dog's tummy and softly lifting as you say the command.

You can also use a short lead to encourage your dog not to travel once standing.

I STARTED THIS TRICK ON: ....

I COMPLETED THIS TRICK BY: ....

THE TRICKS

Now your dog is happily sitting, staying, lying down, standing and giving his or her paw on cue, together you can head for the bright lights of superstardom! Stock up on those tasty treats and brush up on your enthusiastic 'good boy's and 'good girl's – it's trick time.

WAVE

| ALL | 5 DAYS | TASTY TREATS | SIT, STAY, PAW |

If you've taught your dog to give you her paw then you should find this trick fairly simple. I love teaching this one as most dogs pick it up pretty quickly but it looks great and gets lots of laughs.

HOW TO START

Start with your dog sitting in front of you.

HOW TO DO

- Ask your dog to give you her paw. Once you have it in your hand, let go and repeat the command, but this time when you signal for her to raise her paw, bring your hand slightly further back so she has to reach forward to your hand. She will naturally wave it to try to make contact with you. As soon as her paw is raised tell her 'good' and give her a treat.

- Repeat until she has raised her paw consistently about 10 times, then add the command **wave** as she is doing it. Once her paw is where you want it, add 'good'. Try to have her hold that for just a second then catch her paw before she puts it back down. As soon as her paw is in your hand give her the treat. (Do not give her the treat if her paw is back on the ground, as this will confuse her about what she's being expected to perform.)

TIP

Try to build on the time your dog's paw is in the air before you catch it, making sure to tell her 'good' when she is swiping the air trying to make contact. Build the time slowly so she understands what she is doing.

I STARTED THIS TRICK ON: ....

I COMPLETED THIS TRICK BY: ....

COVER YOUR EYES

ALL	3 WEEKS	TASTY TREATS, SURGICAL TAPE/ POST-IT NOTE	SIT, STAY, DOWN

This is one of those tricks used time and again in films and TV, where the dog hides his eyes by putting his paw on his muzzle, either to look shy or so he doesn't have to watch something. My favourite memory of teaching this trick was for 102 Dalmatians with a dog called Lala who played Oddball. It took a little time to teach, but once she'd got it, it was heart-meltingly cute! This is an advanced trick, so don't expect your dog to perform this flawlessly in your first session – just keep practising.

HOW TO START

- You can train this in a sitting or lying-down position. I think lying is easier but some dogs will learn just as fast in a sit.

- You will need something you can place on your dog's muzzle that will prompt him to swipe at it. You can use a piece of surgical tape – or a Post-it note has been a favourite of mine! Of course, do not use any heavy-duty tape that might hurt your dog when it comes off.

HOW TO DO

- Place the tape or Post-it note on your dog's muzzle. Your dog will swipe at it with his paw. As soon as he does this, immediately say 'good' and give him a treat. Take the tape or Post-it note off and then repeat the above. At first, he may swipe just towards the tape. This should be rewarded. But as soon as he touches his nose then give him a super excited 'good boy'.

- After he's swiped at the tape/Post-it note and you've told him 'good' about 10 times consistently, you can add the cue, **cover**, as you place the tape or note on his nose. This will really get him thinking and excited about what he's doing.

- Once your dog is consistently swiping the tape, repeat the above steps and ask him to **cover** but do not actually put the tape on his nose. Hopefully, he will

swipe at his nose straightaway. You can touch the spot the tape was on to give him an extra cue if needed. If that doesn't work then go back to using the tape for a few more sessions.

- Once he is managing the trick with the word **cover** and without the tape being on his nose, throw in the word 'stay' when your dog swipes his nose and encourage him to keep his paw there.

TIP

If your dog does not swipe the tape completely off then remove it for him – you need to be rewarding him every time he does the required behaviour, so you don't want him to carry on doing the action without being rewarded.

I STARTED THIS TRICK ON: ....

I COMPLETED THIS TRICK BY: ....

SALUTE

ALL

1–2 WEEKS

TASTY TREATS, SURGICAL TAPE/ POST-IT NOTE

SIT, STAY, PAW

This trick involves your dog raising her paw up to touch the side of her head as if she is saluting. It is similar to 'cover your eyes' and is quite an advanced trick, so don't expect too much from your dog too soon.

HOW TO START

This needs to be taught with your dog in the 'sit' position. As with 'Cover your eyes', you'll need a Post-it note or a piece of tape – something you can place on your dog which will be easy for her to remove and won't hurt her when it comes off.

HOW TO DO

• Put your Post-it note or piece of tape on your dog's head just above her eye and say '**salute**'. She will raise her paw to remove it. Say 'good' as soon as her paw is beside her face. Keep doing this until she is reliably raising her paw.

- Next, gently touch your dog's head in the place you were previously putting the tape and ask her to **salute**. If she performs the trick then reward her with 'good' and a treat; if she doesn't then go back to using the Post-it note/tape again. You do not need to ask her to hold the paw for any length of time as this should be a short, sharp movement.

TIP

Sometimes dogs get a little lazy with raising the paw high enough, so be sure to only reward them if their paw touches their forehead. It may be you need to go back to using the tape once in a while to get the strong high salute.

I STARTED THIS TRICK ON: ....

I COMPLETED THIS TRICK BY: ....

CRAWL

| ALL | 2–4 WEEKS | TASTY TREATS | SIT, DOWN |

Another trick that is used a lot in films, this one will have your dog moving low along the ground to look stealthy. This isn't as hard as you might think, but it looks pretty impressive! I remember teaching this for the 2005 film Lassie. The dog actor in question had to dramatically crawl under a fence to escape!

HOW TO START

Ask your dog to lie down, then crouch in front of him with a treat in your hand.

HOW TO DO

- Show your dog the treat, then close it in your hand and place your fist in front of his nose. Say the word '**crawl**' and, keeping your hand low against the ground, very slowly bring it back towards you. Only move your hand gradually so as to encourage tiny steps; if you pull your hand away quickly your dog will get up.

- As soon as he has shuffled the tiniest amount, reward him with the treat and say 'good'. Make sure you are only rewarding him when he is in the down position and that he stays in this position at all times.

- Repeat several times. Then you can start to increase the distance between you, always keeping the treat low and making sure to build the distance up gradually, until eventually you can just say the words 'down' and '**crawl**' and your dog will come towards you without you having to physically lead him with the treat.

TIP

If your dog sits up, simply ask him to lie down and try again, making sure you move your hand very slowly and you're keeping it low to the ground at all times.

I STARTED THIS TRICK ON: ....

I COMPLETED THIS TRICK BY: ....

GO TO A MARK

ALL

1–3 WEEKS

TASTY TREATS,
BLOCK OF WOOD/
BIG, HEAVY BOOK

SIT, STAY,
PAW

This is quite an easy trick for when you want your dog to go and stand at a particular point, or a 'mark', as it's called in animal training. I've used this trick in pretty much every film I've ever worked on, but my favourite memory is when we filmed Lassie; *instead of standing on the mark, my dog ran in, picked it up and ran off with it!*

HOW TO START

You'll need an object for the '**mark**'; something which is big enough for your dog's front feet to comfortably fit on, and which is just high enough for her to have to make a step up onto, so she realises there is a difference between the mark and the ground. I'd suggest a sturdy block of wood or a big solid book. Position the mark about one foot away from you and your dog.

HOW TO DO

- Hold a treat in your hand, then ask your dog to 'mark' and use the treat in your hand to guide her on to the block of wood or book. When she puts both her front paws on the block, tell her 'good' straight away and reward her. Then call her off the mark (in any direction, it doesn't matter).

- Repeat, at first guiding her to the mark, then standing behind it so that she is doing the behaviour of her own accord and not because she is following the treat. Always remember to give your dog a nice big 'good' and the treat when she gets it right.

- Once you are confident your dog knows the trick well, you can advance it by building the distance between you, and making the mark smaller and flatter.

TIP

Repetition is the key to this! Keeping your dog standing on the mark saying '**good mark**' is helpful, along with giving her plenty of treats for staying there.

If your dog won't step on the mark, make the mark bigger

so that there's more chance she must step onto it rather than dance around it. If she's really struggling, you can gently lift her paws up onto the mark, but try to avoid this if you can as you'll have much more success rewarding her for making the choice to do it herself. You will probably find that, so long as you are encouraging with food, eventually she will put at least one paw on. Reward this, as it will encourage two paws next time.

I STARTED THIS TRICK ON: ....

I COMPLETED THIS TRICK BY: ....

COME EASY

ALL

1–3 WEEKS

TASTY TREATS

STAND, STAY

This trick is for when you want your dog to walk very slowly towards you. I used this a lot with Hugo, the dog who played Fang in the Harry Potter *series, because – as* Harry Potter *fans will know – even though Fang is a very large Mastiff, he's a big baby so often needed to look a bit cowardly! Having Hugo walk slowly made him seem a bit nervous and suspicious about a situation.*

HOW TO START

Get your dog to stand and stay, then walk a little distance away from them, about 2m/6 ½ft, and face them.

HOW TO DO

- Ask your dog to come to you by saying '**come easy**', but make your tone of voice very gentle. If your dog comes slowly then praise and reward him with a treat. If he comes too fast then go back to the beginning of the trick and try again.

- I find it useful to vary the stopping point so the dog doesn't anticipate you always being the end point and hurry to get there. To do this, ask your dog to **come easy** and then, after he's taken a couple of slow steps, ask him to stay. If he stays when asked, go to him and reward him. Do it again, making sure to always go to him rather than letting him run over to you for his treat and praise.

- After a few goes, your dog should understand that you want him to walk slowly, so you can get him to walk more than a few steps before you ask him to 'stay'. Eventually, you won't need to ask him to stay and go in to reward him, you can get him to walk slowly all the way to you.

TIP

If at any point your dog speeds up, then don't reward him; he'll get confused. Just start the trick again.

I STARTED THIS TRICK ON: ....

I COMPLETED THIS TRICK BY: ....

WALK BACKWARDS

ALL

3 WEEKS

TASTY TREATS

GO TO A MARK,
STAY

This is a quite an advanced trick which involves your dog backing away from you. It's used in films and TV to pretend the dog is trying to get an actor's attention, or to convey that she's scared. Like 'come easy', this was a trick Hugo – the dog actor who played Fang – in the Harry Potter *series had to be very familiar with because he was meant to be a big scaredy-cat(/dog!). If you're familiar with the scene where Fang has to back away from Aragog and the spiders in* Harry Potter and the Chamber of Secrets *then that's a good example of this trick in action!*

HOW TO START

It's often easier to teach this in a narrow space such as a hallway – the idea being that your dog won't be tempted to turn around to face the way you are asking them to go, and it helps them to back up in a straight line. Start by facing your dog, with both of you standing.

- Hold a treat in an open palm under your dog's chin. She will step back to eat it. Just ask for one step at a time at this stage. Repeat, moving your hand back as your dog steps back so that she has to take two steps back to get the treat, and so on and so forth. Make sure to say 'good' as she gets the treat.

- After she's taken about three steps, add the cue **back up**. Make sure you don't use your body to push your dog back – she needs to take the steps herself.

- When she's taking 5 or 6 steps back before you give her the reward, you can try adding a little distance between you and your dog. Ask her to **back up** and still walk towards her, but build up a gap between you. As you build the distance, your dog may want to cheat and turn around. If she does this, go back to a distance she was managing and start to rebuild.

- When you've built a distance between you and your dog of about 90cm/3ft, you can start standing still and asking your dog to '**back up**', so she gets out of the habit of needing you to walk towards her to encourage her to go backwards. Once your dog has backed up far enough, go to your dog and reward her – do not call her forward to you, as then you will be rewarding her for running to you, not for backing away.

- Do not push this trick too much as your dog will start to lose form and will become confused; I'd say don't ask your dog to back up for more than 3m/10ft.

TIP

If your dog starts going sideways, or 'crabbing', as trainers call it, you are probably adding distance too quickly. Reduce the distance until you're getting a nice straight line again.

I STARTED THIS TRICK ON: ....

I COMPLETED THIS TRICK BY: ....

HEAD DOWN

ALL

3–5 DAYS

TASTY TREATS

SIT, DOWN

One of my favourite times teaching this trick was to the puppy playing Oddball in 102 Dalmatians: *she had to put her head down on the ground in order to look a bit subdued after she'd found out she didn't have any spots!*

HOW TO START

Ask your dog to lie down (see page 29). Kneel or stand in front of him, depending on how big he is.

HOW TO DO

- Put a treat in your fingers and make sure your dog knows it's there. Hold the treat in front of his nose, then take it steadily down to the floor. Your dog should follow the treat down and make contact with the ground. As soon as his head touches the ground, say **'head down'**, give him the treat and say 'good'.

- Once he's got this bit, go back to the starting position and this time put the treat in a closed hand. I tuck it under my thumb so I can use my fingers to point to the floor.

- Bring your hand away from his nose so he is not chasing the treat. Say '**head down**' as your hand descends. As soon as his chin touches the floor, reward him. As you go in to reward, try to encourage him to keep his head down by using your other hand as a visual cue, keeping it low with your palm down. Keep your hand with the treat in even lower.

- Once you've mastered this, you can ask your dog to lower his head from a sitting position (a trick used in films when the dog is supposed to be feeling guilty). He might lie down, in which case start again and move the treat towards the floor more slowly.

TIP

If your dog is struggling with this, you can put your free hand on the top of his head and – very gently – push down as your other hand takes the treat down to the floor. Another option that has worked for me in the past is to hold a sheet of cardboard in front of my face. If you do this, your dog should lower his head to look at you from under it.

I STARTED THIS TRICK ON: ....

I COMPLETED THIS TRICK BY: ....

POP HEAD UP

| ALL | 2 DAYS | TASTY TREATS | SIT, DOWN, HEAD DOWN |

This is a classic trick we use in films, where the dog looks a little forlorn with her head on the ground – but then hears something exciting and pops her head up. Your dog will need to confidently know the head down trick before attempting this one.

HOW TO START

Ask your dog to lie down and put her head down.
Kneel in front of her.

HOW TO DO

- Put a treat in front of her nose – making sure she's spotted it – then raise your hand up, luring her head up with it. As you do this, say '**head up**'. As soon as she's done it say 'good' and give her the treat.

- Make sure you don't raise your hand up too high. If you do, you will probably find your dog jumps to her feet – don't reward her for this. Your hand raise needs to be a slow and subtle movement. Ask her to lie back down and to put her head down. Your hand should only rise a few inches off the ground. Reward her with the treat only if she stays in the down position, and say the word 'good'.

I STARTED THIS TRICK ON: ....

I COMPLETED THIS TRICK BY: ....

CROSS LEGS

ALL   2–4 WEEKS   TASTY TREATS   STAY, DOWN, PAW

Before you imagine your dog crossing his legs in the human sense, this trick asks your dog to lie down and cross his paws over each other. This is a sweet trick, and relatively easy if you've taught your dog to give his paw, although it takes quite a bit of practice. Don't worry, by the way, about your dog confusing cross legs with paw once he understands this one. Once he's consistently performing this trick to 'cross your legs', take him through the 'paw' steps a few times to reinforce the difference.

HOW TO START

Ask your dog to lie down, then crouch in front of him.

HOW TO DO

- Ask for his paw. When your dog puts his paw in your hand tell him 'good' and reward him.

- Repeat, but this time move your receiving hand slightly closer to your dog's other leg, so that when you ask him for his 'paw' it overlaps slightly with the other one when up in the air. Continue to reward him each time he places his paw in your hand.

- Next, start to lower your hand so that the paw crosses all the way over the other leg. Eventually, make the movement of asking for his paw, but take your hand away completely so your dog puts his paw down on the floor, crossing his paws. Don't forget to reward every step.

- Once the crossing is happening regularly, replace the word 'paw' with '**cross legs**'.

I STARTED THIS TRICK ON: ....

I COMPLETED THIS TRICK BY: ....

TOUCH OBJECT WITH NOSE

ALL

3 DAYS

TASTY TREATS,
TARGET STICK
(OPTIONAL)

SIT, STAY

This is a trick you can use to get your dog to put her nose on an object of your choice. You can buy a target stick to help teach this trick, or you can make your own: in the past I've used a ping pong ball on a stick. However, the classic and easiest method is to use your hand, as then you can practise this anywhere without needing a prop.

HOW TO START

Ask your dog to either stand or sit.

HOW TO DO

- Hold your hand with your fingers splayed out and offer your hand to your dog. Most dogs will come forward to your hand. The second your dog's nose touches your hand say 'good' and give her a treat. After she's done this a few times and understands the behaviour expected of her, ask her to **target** when you open your hand. Try to have her come to you to target rather than you going to her.

- Once she has learnt this on your hand you can transfer the cue onto other things by showing her what you want to target. For example, for the film *Patrick* (out in 2018), I needed my little pug actor to touch the fridge with his nose so it looked as if he was opening it. Once he knew how to target my hand, I took him close to the fridge, asked him to **target**, then told him 'good' and rewarded him. You can do the same for any object. Always be quick with your positive reward.

TIP

Try not to hold the reward in the hand you are using as the target, as this will distract her or encourage her to lick instead of touching.

I STARTED THIS TRICK ON: ....

I COMPLETED THIS TRICK BY: ....

TOUCH OBJECT WITH PAW

ALL

3 DAYS

TASTY TREATS,
TARGET STICK
(OPTIONAL)

SIT, STAY,
PAW

This is similar to the previous trick, except you're asking your dog to touch an object with his paw rather than his nose. If you've taught your dog to give you his paw then you should find this relatively simple. I've trained this trick for many occasions, most often when a dog needs to hit a remote control to change the channel on the TV.

HOW TO START

Ask your dog to sit, then warm him up by asking him to give you his paw. Reward him as you usually would.

HOW TO DO

- Ask your dog to give you his paw again, but this time back away slightly and leave the paw for a second before you catch it in your hand. Reward him.

- Place something slightly in front and to the side of him. I use something that is just below the dog's shoulder height, so not too high or low.

- Ask him to raise his paw. He should naturally want to then rest it on the item. As soon as he touches it, say 'good', reward him and add the new cue, **foot**. Once he's done this successfully a few times, change to a different item so he really understands what he is doing.

- The challenge then is to ask him to stay before having him walk to the item and put his paw on it. Point to the item you want him to touch. As he approaches it give the cue **foot**. As soon as he places his foot on the object reward him, then keep practising until he is confidently touching the object each time.

TIP

Make sure you reward your dog when he has his paw on the item, not when he puts it back on the ground.

I STARTED THIS TRICK ON: ....

I COMPLETED THIS TRICK BY: ....

NUDGE

| ALL | 1–2 WEEKS | TASTY TREATS, A PLASTIC BOWL OR EQUIVALENT NON-FRAGILE OBJECT, DOORSTOP | – |

This trick involves your dog pushing an object with her nose. It's one of the most difficult tricks in the book to teach, but worth the effort.

HOW TO START

I prefer to teach this standing up, with the dog standing to one side of me. You'll need a treat and a robust object that you don't mind getting slobbered on – a plastic bowl is perfect.

HOW TO DO

- The idea here is to place the treat under the object, so that your dog will nudge it to get the treat. You have to make this very easy and positive to start with, otherwise she will give up straight away. I use a doorstop or other wedge under the bowl so I can raise it slightly on one side. Place the treat in the crevice so that the dog can see there is a treat hiding under the bowl, and it's easy for her to retrieve it. As she gets the treat, say the word '**nudge**' and praise her. Do this several times. At this stage of training the trick, the treat should only come from under the object – not your hand.

- Once she's mastered this, place the treat slightly further under the bowl to make it a little harder for her to get to. She should then flip the bowl with her nose to get to the treat. Again, do this several times to keep it very positive, always saying '**nudge**' and praising her as she gets the treat.

- The next stage is to take away the wedge, but let your dog see you put the treat under the bowl. As she comes in to get the treat tell her '**nudge**'. As soon as her nose hits the bowl, lift it up so she can get the treat. Keep doing this, getting her to nudge the bowl for a little longer each time before you lift the bowl to let her retrieve the treat. Once she understands **nudge**,

you don't need to put a treat under the object. Instead, as soon as she nudges it, give her the treat from your hand. Every fourth or fifth time, put the treat back underneath the bowl to reinforce the nudge.

- The nudge can be transferred onto many objects, and even people!

I STARTED THIS TRICK ON: ....

I COMPLETED THIS TRICK BY: ....

BOW

ALL   1 WEEK   TASTY TREATS   –

This can be used for a polite bow; to make it look as if your dog is saying prayers; or playing with you. I also used it recently on the film Patrick *(out in 2018) to make it look as if the dog playing Patrick was stretching after he'd got out of bed.*

HOW TO START

You will need to have your dog standing on all fours and facing you. (If he is sitting he will lie down instead of just his front end going down.) I prefer to remain standing myself, rather than kneeling for this one, as being too low may encourage your dog to lie down.

- Hold a treat in front of your dog's nose. Take the treat down to the ground, keeping it close to his body. As you do this, say '**bow**'. As soon as he starts to lower his front you can reward him by giving him the treat and saying 'good'.

- Keep doing this little by little, keeping the treat close to your dog's body and rewarding him for going down a little further each time. What you are aiming for is to have his elbows on the ground and his bottom in the air. As ever, ensure he is always rewarded in the bow position, not once he has popped up into a standing position.

- After your dog has performed the trick properly three to five times, you should be able to have him follow the cue, **bow**, without luring him with food in your hand. You should still use a downward hand motion as a visual cue.

TIP

You may find that your dog wants to lie down when you take your hand down to the floor. You can try to stand slightly side-on to him and pop your arm under his tummy, using your other hand to lure his nose down to the ground, thus showing him the bow position. I do prefer to work from the front for this trick, but side-on is OK too.

If your dog is persistently lying down, then look for much less before you reward, such as just a lowering of the nose, and build towards the bow more slowly.

I STARTED THIS TRICK ON: ....

I COMPLETED THIS TRICK BY: ....

BEG

SMALL/MEDIUM   2–4 WEEKS   TASTY TREATS   SIT, STAY

The idea with this trick is to have your dog's hindquarters stay on the ground, cutely raising her front paws whilst keeping a nice straight spine – a trick used time and again in adverts for dog food! Large dogs may find this difficult as they are top heavy, and so some may not want to make the effort, but they are still capable of doing it.

HOW TO START

Your dog needs to start off in a sitting position. Some trainers stand behind the dog to train this, but I like to stand in front of them.

HOW TO DO

- Hold a treat in front of your dog's nose and raise it up over her head. Once she is following the treat by moving her head backwards, give it to her and say 'good'.

- Start again, this time raising the treat ever so slightly higher to see if you can get her to raise her front paws slightly to get it. Do not move it too fast or too high, as this will cause your dog to stand. You almost want your dog to roll back slightly for the treat. The key here is to support her paws as they come up – do this with your hand that isn't holding the treat. Supporting her paws will help build her confidence that she can steady herself. As you lure her back use the word '**beg**' or '**sit up**' – whichever you'd rather.

- After completing the trick five times with your hands there as a support, gradually start to offer less support so that she has to balance herself for a few seconds, before you quickly support the raised front paws with your arm or hands to reinforce that it's the begging position you're after. Say 'good' and reward her.

- Once your dog is able to balance by herself, back away whilst saying 'stay'. Then rush forward to support her paws, say 'good' and reward her whilst her paws are still up.

TIP

When you're at the backing-away stage, be sure to hold
the treat high as you back away – your dog might bring
her body down if you hold it low. Don't push the time
too long, as you don't want her to topple and make it a
negative experience.

I STARTED THIS TRICK ON: ....

I COMPLETED THIS TRICK BY: ....

SPIN

| ALL | 2 DAYS | TASTY TREATS | STAND |

This is probably the easiest trick for your dog to learn; encouraging him to spin in a circle and follow his tail.

HOW TO START

Face your dog and ask him to stand. Have a treat ready in your hand.

HOW TO DO

- Put the treat near your dog's nose. Say the cue '**spin**', then slowly lure your dog round in a full circle. Once he is back where he started, reward him with the treat and say 'good' – make sure he has done the full turn and that you're not rewarding him halfway round.

- Repeat this several times, so your dog understands the behaviour he is being rewarded for is spinning in a circle, and you know that he's not just following the

food. You can check this by using your empty hand to visually lead your dog round and keeping the treat in your other hand.

- As he improves, you can ask him to do faster circles simply by moving your hand faster – this will make him look like he is chasing his tail. You can then start building some distance between you, so you don't have to stand over your dog to get him to do the movement.

I STARTED THIS TRICK ON: ....

I COMPLETED THIS TRICK BY: ....

SPEAK

SMALL/MEDIUM   2–5 WEEKS   TASTY TREATS   –

A dog barking as if she's talking to another dog or human is a trick used in pretty much every film where a dog is featured. It's quite simple to teach, so long as you can manufacture an opportunity to get your dog to do it and reward her at the same time.

HOW TO START

There are several ways to teach this trick. Have a think about what naturally makes your dog bark and adapt the ideas below to suit this. Make sure you have some treats ready in your hand or pocket.

HOW TO DO

- If your dog barks at a doorbell or door knock, take her to the front door and knock or ring the bell. Just before you do this, say '**speak**', so your dog gradually learns you are giving her a command. As soon as your dog barks, reward her with the treat and say 'good'. Repeat this a few times, then leave out the door knocking or bell ringing and see if she will do the trick on the **speak** cue. If she doesn't, go back to knocking or ringing, but make sure she hears you say '**speak**' before you do it.

- Alternatively, if your dog is toy motivated, you can excite her with a toy whilst saying '**speak**', and then as soon as she's made a little noise you can throw the toy to her as a reward.

- My preferred method is to set up a baby gate or similar. Put your dog behind the gate and walk away. As soon as she makes a whimper, run back and give her the treat whilst saying '**speak**'. Each time you get your dog to repeat this trick, encourage her to make a bit more noise by leaving it a few more seconds after the first little noise – a grunt or whine will usually turn into a bark eventually, and you want to be rewarding a bark as quickly as possible so your dog isn't confused.

- Keep going until she reliably barks on cue. Once she is doing this, bring her to your side of the gate and ask her to speak without walking away. If she doesn't bark first time round (which is common) then go back to putting her behind the gate for a few more tries.

TIP

Once you've trained your dog to do this, it's important that you then only reward them if you've given the speak cue. Dogs can enjoy this one a bit too much, which can become a problem! If they start offering the bark when you don't want them to, you can try the opposite and reward and teach them '**enough**' or '**quiet**' when they aren't barking.

I STARTED THIS TRICK ON: ....

I COMPLETED THIS TRICK BY: ....

COCK LEG

| ALL | 2–4 WEEKS | TASTY TREATS, A FEW THICK BOOKS | STAND, STAY |

This is just in case you ever have the urge to get your dog to mimic peeing! I most recently had to teach this to a Collie cross called Flint for a National Lottery advert; he had to cock his leg on James Blunt singing in a mirror – it was hysterical!

HOW TO START

You'll need a large book for this trick, something like a big dictionary that has enough pages in it so your dog will have to lift his leg to touch the top of it (but don't start off too high – your dog needs to be able to reach the top in the beginning). Ask your dog to stand and then kneel or stand in front of him, depending on how big he is. Place the book on the floor beside your dog's back leg.

HOW TO DO

- The idea is to get your dog to put his back leg on the book. You can start by just placing his back foot on it and then reward him for standing in that position with a treat and by saying 'good'.

- Once he is doing that nicely, start again – always picking the same side to put the book next to, as your dog may become confused if you change sides. Instead of placing his foot on the book this time, gently touch the inside of his leg and see if he will raise his leg himself and place it on the book. Reward him with a treat and a 'good' as soon as he starts to lift his leg. Start adding the verbal cue of **hike** or **lift your leg**. Keep repeating the action and the cue – each time encouraging him to lift his leg a little higher. (Be patient – this stage takes the longest.)

- The aim is for him to eventually lift his leg onto the book himself. Make sure to reward him as soon as his leg touches the book and not when he has put it back on the ground, or he will be confused about what behaviour he is supposed to be performing.

Once he's placed his leg on the book a good few times, encourage him to 'stay'.

- Once he is doing this well, add another book. He will start feeling for it and raising his leg higher to hit the top of the books. Don't forget that each stage needs lots of praise and reward. Keep adding books to get height until it really looks like he is lifting his leg to pee. When he has mastered it, you can replace the books with other objects.

I STARTED THIS TRICK ON: ....

I COMPLETED THIS TRICK BY: ....

YAWN

ALL

4–8 WEEKS

TASTY TREATS

SIT, STAY

*Now, this one is not the easiest trick to teach, as you need to wait for the behaviour in order to reward it, so it can take a bit of time! You can help it along by telling your dog '**good yawn**' each time you see her do it. The quickest of the dogs I've trained to pick it up was a scruffy crossbreed called Mojo. When he yawned he made the funniest sound – I think he enjoyed the laugh he got each time he did it, which encouraged him to pick up this trick faster.*

HOW TO START

Dogs often yawn if they're confused. So, ask her to sit, then sit in front of her with her favourite toy or treat and do nothing!

HOW TO DO

- Your dog will hopefully look at you, very confused and waiting for a command. She may offer a trick – if she

does this, ignore it. You'll see the cogs start to turn at this point, as she wonders what on earth you're doing. There is a high chance that if you wait she will yawn.

- When she does yawn, you need to be very quick and precise about telling her '**good yawn**', then reward her.

Keep doing this. Patience is the key here – this is what we call 'shaping a natural behaviour'. I often find that when I'm teaching a new trick to a dog, she will yawn if she's a little unsure about what she's doing. Any time your dog does this, say '**good yawn**' and reward with a treat, to encourage her to do it more in future.

TIP

If your dog wanders off when you're trying to encourage a yawn, bring her back and ask her to sit and stay. (If she does this a few times, it is good to do a separate sit and stay session to reinforce these behaviours.)

Yawns are contagious to dogs, as they are to people, so you yawning can also encourage your dog to yawn! Your dog slightly opening her mouth and licking her lips can be signs she is about to yawn.

I STARTED THIS TRICK ON: ....

I COMPLETED THIS TRICK BY: ....

LIE ON SIDE

ALL

2 WEEKS

TASTY TREATS,
COMFY SURFACE

DOWN, STAY,
STAND

*I'm often asked to use this trick for shots of dogs sleeping,
as you can position them so you can't see if their eyes are
open and it looks like they are asleep. It also forms the
basis of roll over (see page 103).*

HOW TO START

Make sure you're somewhere the ground is comfortable,
then ask your dog to lie down and reward him for this.
Ideally, one of your dog's hips will be relaxed on the
ground. If it isn't, tell him to stand and then ask him to lie
down again. Hopefully one hip will be on the ground this
time, but if not you can help him out by gently rolling him
onto one hip yourself.

Kneel in front of your dog and pop a treat in your hand.

HOW TO DO

- Move the hand with the treat in towards your dog's shoulder. Whatever hip he is resting on is going to be the side he lies flat on, so make sure you're taking the treat towards the shoulder that will not end up on the floor. This will lure his head round, which should cause him to roll onto his side. It may help to gently touch his shoulder, to encourage him to go onto his side. As he does this, say '**on your side**'. Once he is flat on his side reward him straight away and tell him 'good'.

- Repeat, but this time, before you reward him, try to encourage him to put his head on the floor by moving your hand with the treat in to where you want his head to go. Once he's done this, say 'good', then transfer the treat to your other hand. Use the hand without the treat to get him to follow into a flat, straight position (as opposed to being curled up). Quickly reward him with the treat.

- Once he's doing this quite happily, you can then build up the length of time that he is on his side before he gets the treat. Repeat the steps above then ask him to stay in that position.

- You can then try backing away from him. As you back away, make the same movements with the hand you've been luring with as a visual cue, and say '**on your side**'. If he flips over or gets up as you back away, go back to him, ask him to lie down, repeat the steps above and try again.

TIP

Once you've built up a bit of distance, you will probably find that your dog will want to roll up when you go to reward him. Ask him to go back on his side and reward him in that position as often as you can. Make sure you don't reward him when he's back up, or he'll get confused about what behaviour he should be performing.

I STARTED THIS TRICK ON: ....

I COMPLETED THIS TRICK BY: ....

LIE ON BACK

SMALL/MEDIUM   2–4 WEEKS   TASTY TREATS, COMFY SURFACE   SIT, DOWN, LIE ON SIDE, STAY

This isn't the easiest trick to teach, as some dogs find it slightly odd and want to roll onto one side for balance. Be sure your dog is happy and confident to try it – if she's not, then stop! Make sure the surface is very comfortable. I often use a duvet, or a pillow for smaller dogs, as you can make a little channel-like support for your dog to lie in.
Do not try this trick with large dogs as it can cause them tummy problems. Also, don't teach this trick if your dog has just had a lot to eat or drink.

HOW TO START

Ask your dog to lie down on her side, then kneel down in front of her near to her head.

HOW TO DO

- Next, slowly move a treat from her shoulder over her

face, whilst saying '**over**', so she follows the treat and rolls onto her back. As soon as she is on her back tell her 'good' and give her the treat. Offer her the treat so that she moves her head onto one side and can eat safely.

- Repeat the steps above and try to build the time she is on her back by saying 'stay' before you give her the treat. After your dog is doing this confidently, you can stop using the treat to make her move and just use the hand movement and cue, **over**.

TIP

Remember, this is not a favourite trick for some dogs – if you think your dog is distressed do not continue. Also make sure you are giving her lots and lots of super 'good girl's for getting it right.

I STARTED THIS TRICK ON: ....

I COMPLETED THIS TRICK BY: ....

ROLL OVER

SMALL/MEDIUM

1–2 WEEKS

TASTY TREATS,
COMFY SURFACE

SIT, DOWN, LIE
ON SIDE, STAY

*Once you have taught your dog to lie on his side (page 97),
this is a fairly easy trick to teach. Once again, do not try this
trick with large dogs because it can give them a problem
with their tummy. Also, don't teach this if your dog
has just had a lot to eat or drink.*

HOW TO START

Ask your dog to lie down and reward him. I always reward
each step of this trick to keep him focused.

HOW TO DO

- The next step is to ask your dog to lie on his side.
  Reward him again when he does this. Put a treat in
  your hand, and move it from above your dog's shoulder
  – the one not on the floor – up and back, so that he has
  to move onto his back to look at it. Continue to move

the treat so that your dog rolls onto his other side and then follows it until he is back on his tummy, then immediately say 'good' and give him the treat. I find it easier to then release him with 'OK' (see page 22) and start the process again, rather than have him roll back.

- Once your dog has done the above five times, add the words '**roll over**'. Once he understands and is rolling fully over you can slowly start to back away. Ask him to lie down and stay, then ask him to '**roll over**', making the same hand movement as when you were getting him to follow the treat. You can then try adding a couple more commands of **roll over** and go for two or three consecutive rolls.

TIP

Remember to reward him once he's back in the down position, and tell him 'good' for each step of the process he manages correctly.

I STARTED THIS TRICK ON: ....

I COMPLETED THIS TRICK BY: ....

CATCH

ALL   1 WEEK   TASTY TREATS, BALL OR SOFT TOY   SIT, STAY

This is a fun trick where you get your dog to catch objects as you pretend to be clumsy. It can take a bit of time for your dog to learn, depending on their eye–mouth coordination, but it's worth the practice once he gets it.

HOW TO START

Have your dog sit in front of you, and hold a treat in your hand.

HOW TO DO

- First of all, just feed your dog the treat, but hold it a little above him so he has to reach up to get it (but not so high any of his feet need to come off the ground).

- Repeat, but this time drop the treat from a very short distance, whilst saying '**catch**'. He is likely to miss

sometimes at first – if he does miss, try to stop him getting the treat off the ground. Instead, pick the treat up and try again. If he catches it, say 'good' and let him munch away.

- Once your dog can consistently catch the treat in mid-air with you dropping it from a low height, start to drop from a slightly higher distance, still saying '**catch**' and 'good' if he gets it. You can progress from there to throwing it to him, but obviously be very gentle!

- You can then start to use a ball or a soft toy. Don't ask him to catch anything heavy or harmful. It should be a straightforward swap, as he now knows the word **catch**. Just remember to reward with 'good' and a treat straight away afterwards.

I STARTED THIS TRICK ON: ....

I COMPLETED THIS TRICK BY: ....

HOLD AN OBJECT

ALL

2–3 WEEKS

TASTY TREATS, RUBBER DUMBBELL OR OTHER DOG TOY

SIT, STAY

This is quite a difficult trick for dogs to learn, as whilst they may happily pick something up, they don't always want to keep hold of it. Make sure you do sessions of this little and often – you want to keep your dog's enthusiasm up. Once she is doing this trick confidently, though, the possibilities are endless: you could ask your dog to hold the Halloween bucket of sweets when visitors come knocking, or even the engagement ring box as you propose! You can then move on to teaching them to bring an object (see page 111), which has many uses of its own.

HOW TO START

Have your dog stand in front of you. You'll need a toy that is made for dogs, such as a dumbbell, as well as some treats (pop these in your pocket – you don't want to keep any in your hand, as you'll distract your dog).

HOW TO DO

- Present the dumbbell to your dog whilst asking her to '**pick it up**'.

- As soon as she puts it in her mouth, or touches it with her mouth in any way, say 'good' and give her a treat. Repeat.

- Once your dog is regularly putting her mouth on the dumbbell, try to increase the time that she has hold of it whilst saying the cue '**hold**'. At first, make sure you keep hold of the dumbbell as well, until her hold on it is established. If your dog chews the toy or pushes it with her feet, just withdraw it and present it again – do not reward for this.

- When she's holding on to it with no problem, start to support less and less of the dumbbell's weight until you can let it go completely and your dog will hold it on her own. At first, reward straight away. Then you can start building up the time your dog has hold of the dumbbell by saying '**hold**' and rewarding after a few seconds, then 10 seconds, then 15, and so on.

TIP

Always use the same object whilst training this. Once your dog understands '**hold**' you can try other objects (but bear in mind weight and fragility – you don't want to give her anything heavy or potentially harmful). She may refuse at first, but keep saying '**hold**' as if she's confidently holding the dumbbell and she will eventually understand.

I STARTED THIS TRICK ON: ....

I COMPLETED THIS TRICK BY: ....

BRING AN OBJECT

ALL	3–4 WEEKS	TASTY TREATS, RUBBER DUMBBELL OR OTHER DOG TOY	HOLD AN OBJECT, STAY

You may have been waiting the whole book to find the trick where you can teach your dog to bring you the paper. Well, here it is! (Although be warned, if you can somehow manage to get him to retrieve it from another room, it will no doubt end up in your lap covered in slobber.) It's not the easiest of tricks, because some dogs can hold an object but don't think they can move with it! But, so long as your dog can confidently hold an object (see page 108), then you stand a good chance.

HOW TO START

Start with the 'Hold an object' training on page 108. Give him the dumbbell (or whatever you taught 'Hold an object' with), then back a couple of steps away from your dog whilst saying 'stay'.

- Ask him to '**hold**' and '**come**'. If he moves towards you without dropping the dumbbell then take it from him, say '**good**', and reward him with a treat and another '**good**'. However, you will probably find that he will drop the dumbbell as he takes his first takes steps towards you. Encourage him to '**pick it up**', then ask him again to 'hold' and 'come'. (If your dog doesn't pick the dumbbell back up, then give it to him whilst saying '**pick it up**' and reward him, then back away and ask him to '**hold**' and '**come**'.)

- Build the distance in tiny steps – don't rush it. It is more important at this stage that he can walk whilst keeping the dumbbell in his mouth than that he can close the distance between you. Over time, you can build the distance between you. Like 'Hold an object', you will be able to transfer the cue to any object.

TIP

Make sure you teach this trick in short sessions and try to end when your dog is on a high, rather than frustrated. If you have a dog that finds it difficult to move with an object in his mouth, then you can place his mark (see

112

page 50) in front of you and ask your dog to go to the mark with the object in his mouth. This also helps with building the distance he will carry it.

I STARTED THIS TRICK ON: ....

I COMPLETED THIS TRICK BY: ....

WATCH AN OBJECT

ALL · 1–3 WEEKS · TASTY TREATS, OBJECT AT YOUR DOG'S SHOULDER HEIGHT · SIT, STAY

*The idea with this one is to have your dog look
at an object instead of looking at you!*

HOW TO START

You'll need a treat and, eventually, something to put it on
that is roughly the shoulder height of your dog, such as a
wooden block or a chair. (Don't put the treat on the floor,
as your dog will be hugely tempted to collect it straight
away!) Ask her to sit and stay.

HOW TO DO

- Show your dog you have a treat. Standing to the side
  of her, hold the treat and when she looks at it, say
  '**watch**' and 'good' and reward her.

- Next, place the treat on the block or chair and stand next to it, keeping your hand close by. Encourage her to watch the treat by saying '**watch**' and pointing. Again, as soon as she looks at it, say 'good' and 'OK', so she can come and get the treat. Make sure you say it with enthusiasm! Also make sure anything you put the treat on is sturdy, as when your dog finally gets to collect it, it should be a nice easy reward for her. Place it about 1 metre/3 feet from your dog (far enough to reduce temptation, but close enough that she keeps focus).

- Once you've done this a few times, she should understand that the idea is to watch the treat, not your hand. This is when you should start taking your hand away. Place the treat on the block or chair, remove your hand and say '**watch**'. At this point, she might cheat and run to steal the treat! Dash in and grab it yourself before she does, or the only trick she'll be learning is that she can get a treat as soon as you back away! Have her sit and stay, then give the **watch** cue again. It is important you tell her both 'stay' and '**watch**'.

- As soon as you have backed a little away from the chair or block, tell her '**watch**' again. The second she watches, tell her 'good' and 'OK' so she can come and collect the treat.

- Eventually, you should be able to put the treat anywhere – including the floor – and have her watch it.

TIP

If she is a real cheat, you can train this on the lead until she sits patiently and watches the treat.

I STARTED THIS TRICK ON: ....

I COMPLETED THIS TRICK BY: ....

STEP UP

ALL	LESS THAN 1 WEEK	TASTY TREATS, AN OBJECT FOR YOUR DOG TO STEP ONTO	SIT, STAY

Once he's mastered this, your dog will be able to put his feet on a variety of objects – and people if you wish! It's not good to do this with any breeds or individual dogs that have genetic hip problems, as it will put strain on those joints.

HOW TO START

Position your dog in front of the object you'd like him to stand on. The object should be of a sensible size and sturdy, so it doesn't move when he rests his weight on it. Have a treat in one hand.

HOW TO DO

- Using the treat, lure your dog up until they step onto the object with their front feet – when they do this, use the words '**put your feet up**'. Tell your dog 'good' and

reward him straight away. Always reward him when his feet are up, not when he's jumped down.

- Repeat until you no longer have to use the treat to lure him and you can just say the **put your feet up** cue. Then give it a go with people instead of the object!

I STARTED THIS TRICK ON: ....

I COMPLETED THIS TRICK BY: ....

STAND UP

SMALL/MEDIUM   1–2 WEEKS   TASTY TREATS   STAND, STAY

This is a classic trick: asking your dog to stand on her hind legs like a person. Make sure your dog is happy to stand and stay on command. Sorry, big dogs – I'm afraid this one isn't suitable for you, as it puts too much weight and pressure on your hips and hind legs.

Similarly, if you're a dog with a long spine, such as a Basset or a Dachshund, or a dog with bad hips, then you should sit this one out too. But for everyone else, there's no harm in giving this one a go – so long as you don't hold the position for too long.

HOW TO START

Ask your dog to stand. Stand in front of her with a treat in your hand.

HOW TO DO

- Make sure your dog is aware of the treat in your hand. Then raise it from her nose up high to the ceiling and slightly over her back – you want her to rise up rather than launch forward. Give her the cue, **stand up**. As she rises, tell her 'good' and give her the treat.

- Keep repeating the trick, every time encouraging your dog to bring her front legs slightly higher off the ground by taking the treat higher – make sure you keep rewarding and praising her.

- Once your dog is confidently standing with a straight back (this will help her balance), try to back away a tiny bit, still holding the treat very high, so she begins to understand you do not need to be there for support.

- If you'd like her to try walking, when she is standing start to bring the treat towards you very slowly. These must be tiny steps, so don't move the treat away too fast or too far. After your dog has taken a couple of steps, reward her and say 'good'. Repeat the trick, and start adding the cue '**walk up**'.

- You may find your dog takes a step and then puts her front feet back on the ground. If she does this, try to support her with your arm under her front legs so she stays upright.

TIP

It's really important not to take the treat too far back or keep it too far forward, or your dog won't be in the right position to balance correctly. It needs to be above her head.

I STARTED THIS TRICK ON: ....

I COMPLETED THIS TRICK BY: ....

JUMP UP AND DOWN

SMALL/MEDIUM   LESS THAN   TASTY TREATS   –
            1 WEEK

This is a fun, easy trick to teach, particularly if you have a lively dog. I would not recommend this for big dogs, however, or dogs with long spines such as Bassets or Dachshunds.

HOW TO START

You'll need a treat in your hand – simply use it to get your dog's attention.

HOW TO DO

- Hold the treat above your dog's head, just out of reach, but not so high that should he stretch to get it he'll miss it – the treat needs to be within his jumping range. You may need to bring the treat down to his nose and then back up to encourage him to make more of an effort to get it. Say '**jump**' as you do this. As he becomes interested, he will rise up. What you're

123

looking for is a stretch and, ideally, a little hop. Once he's done this say 'good' and let him have the treat.

- Repeat, but this time hold the treat a little higher, so he needs to jump up to get it. (Watch your fingers, as dogs can get quite carried away with this one!) Keep repeating, each time gradually increasing the height, but making sure it's always a distance your dog can manage.

- Gradually, you can reduce this to just saying '**jump**' and flicking your hands towards the ceiling as a visual cue. Let your dog jump a few times, so he learns he needs to do it more than once, before giving him a 'good boy' and the reward.

I STARTED THIS TRICK ON: ....

I COMPLETED THIS TRICK BY: ....

HUG

| ALL | 2–3 WEEKS | TASTY TREATS | SIT, STAY, BEG |

This is, of course, an especially rewarding trick to teach! But a word of warning: only teach this to your dog if she's comfortable with physical contact and you know she will not have any issues with the hug. If at any time your dog shows signs of being uncomfortable with having you in her personal space then stop immediately – you don't want to upset her.

You also need to be careful trying this with big dogs because of the pressure it puts on their legs, hips and spine – although that's not to say you can't give it a go (so long as you're confident they won't knock you over!). The biggest dog I've done it with was a fluffy Pyrenean Mountain Dog for the film Finding Neverland. *He had to put his front legs on Johnny Depp's shoulders and dance!*

HOW TO START

Ask your dog to 'sit' and then 'beg'. Kneel or stand in front of your dog depending on her size – you need to be at a height where you can put her front legs on your shoulders.

HOW TO DO

- Once your dog can comfortably hold the beg position for around four seconds, you can start the hug. Face your dog and lean forward. Tell her '**hug**', put your arms around her and let her rest her front legs on your shoulders.

- Straight away, say 'good' and give her a treat. Repeat, but this time leave it a couple of seconds before you reward her. Gradually build the time of the hug, but make sure you don't frustrate your dog. I usually only do it for a couple of seconds.

I STARTED THIS TRICK ON: ....

I COMPLETED THIS TRICK BY: ....

SUPERSTAR DOG

THIS IS TO CERTIFY THAT:

....

has mastered all the tricks in this book
to the best of his/her ability.

DATE:

....

SIGNED BY:

....

(the 'Facilitating Human')